I0896100

Amazing Animals

World Record WILDLIFE

Adding and Subtracting Fractions

Elise Wallace

Consultants

Lisa Ellick, M.A.
Math Specialist,
Norfolk Public Schools

Pamela Estrada, M.S.Ed.
Teacher
Westminster School District

Publishing Credits

Rachelle Cracchiolo, M.S.Ed., *Publisher*
Conni Medina, M.A.Ed., *Managing Editor*
Dona Herweck Rice, *Series Developer*
Emily R. Smith, M.A.Ed., *Series Developer*
Diana Kenney, M.A.Ed., NBCT, *Content Director*
Stacy Monsman, M.A., *Editor*
Kristy Stark, M.A.Ed., *Editor*
Kevin Panter, *Graphic Designer*

Image Credits: Front cover Eamonn McCormack/WireImage; p.1 Eamonn McCormack/WireImage; p.4 Peter Lane/Alamy; p.5 Z5327 Soeren Stache Deutsch Presse Agentur/Newscom; pp6, 7 Alex Segre/Alamy; p.8 Paris Pierce/Alamy; p.9 Chronicle/Alamy; p.10 Columbia Pictures/Ronald Grant Archive/Alamy; p.11 Entertainment Pictures/Alamy; p.12 (bottom left) Granger Academic; p.13 Science Source; p.14 (bottom right) HSNPhotography/iStock; p15 (top) Andrey Khachatryan/ Shutterstock; p.16 (top) Jaap2/iStock; p.16 (bottom) Bill Pugliano/Getty Images; p.20 Superelaks/Alamy; p.24 (top) Hero Images Inc/Alamy; p.25 Lifeman/Alamy; p.26 Sergei Konkov/TASS via Getty Images; p.27 (top) ChameleonsEye/Shutterstock; all other images from iStock and/or Shutterstock.

Teacher Created Materials
5301 Oceanus Drive
Huntington Beach, CA 92649-1030
http://www.tcmpub.com

ISBN 978-1-4258-5813-1
© 2018 Teacher Created Materials, Inc.
Printed by: 590835
Printed in: Taiwan

Table of Contents

World Records

Every four years, the Olympics are held. People cheer for the fastest and strongest athletes. They are awarded with gold medals for their hard work.

People also cheer for small achievements. People can set world records for blowing the biggest bubblegum bubble. They can build the largest house of cards. There's no task or trick too small. Anyone can become the world's greatest.

There are world-record holders in the animal kingdom, too. They deserve to be celebrated! The world is filled with many amazing animals. Some are incredibly big. Others are amazingly small. Some are very fast. Others are very slow. Many animals are unique enough to have a claim to fame. If there were an Animal Olympics, these creatures would surely be gold medalists!

Workers at LEGO Italy set a new record for tallest LEGO structure by building a tower that is 35.05 meters tall.

Three gymnasts accept medals at the 2016 Rio Summer Olympics.

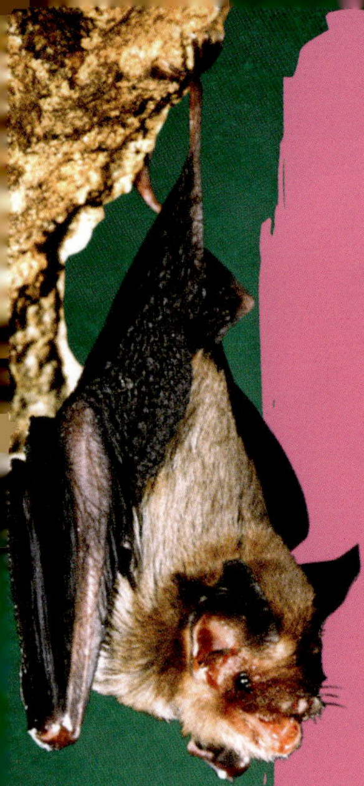

From Miniature to Monstrous

These creatures stomp, scamper, swim, and soar. They range from the world's tiniest creatures to its biggest beasts. Each is a world-record holding animal.

Itty-Bitty Bat

Tiny enough to perch on a pinky finger, the bumblebee bat is the world's smallest bat species. It is a little longer than 1 inch (2.5 centimeters) and weighs about as much as a dime. But, don't be fooled by its size. The bumblebee bat is just as skilled as bigger bats!

Like other bat species, this tiny creature uses **echolocation**. It allows the bat to "see" using sound. When on the hunt, bats send out high-pitched signals. These sounds bounce off things around them. The faster a sound bounces back, the closer something is to the bat. This ability helps them find prey.

Bumblebee bats are **insectivores**, which means that they eat insects. Like other bats, bumblebee bats hunt at night. This species lives primarily in Thailand, in limestone caves.

Today, bumblebee bats are in danger. They are a vulnerable species. Some tourists have disturbed their **habitats**. Their caves must be protected for this species to continue to take flight.

Let's Explore Math

A bumblebee bat weighs about $\frac{7}{100}$ of an ounce.

1. Does a bumblebee bat weigh more than or less than $\frac{1}{2}$ ounce? How do you know?
2. Imagine that scientists weigh 2 bumblebee bats. Which estimate best describes the total weight? Explain your reasoning.

    A. less than $\frac{1}{2}$ ounce

    B. greater than $\frac{1}{2}$ ounce, less than 1 ounce

    C. greater than 1 ounce

A bumblebee bat emerges from its cave.

bumblebee bat

Micro Reptile

Micro reptiles are among the tiniest **reptiles** in the world. One species of chameleon is the smallest known micro reptile on the planet. It is about the same size as a bumblebee bat. The species is called *Brookesia micra*. It was discovered a few years ago on Madagascar, an African island.

Why is it so small? Scientists think that the reptile's size may be a result of its home. They believe that some animals shrink in size hundreds of times when they have small habitats, such as islands. This is called *island dwarfism*. In such conditions, scientists think some creatures slowly produce smaller offspring. Smaller animals need fewer resources, such as food and shelter.

The *Brookesia micra* was discovered along with three other chameleon species. Of the four species, the *Brookesia micra* is the smallest. That's why *micra* is part of its name. The word *micra* comes from the Greek word *mikros*, which means small!

Also known as leaf chameleons, these reptiles are active during the day. They sleep in trees at night. Like other chameleons, their eyes have special features. One eye can look to the left while the other can look up!

leaf chameleon

Male leaf chameleons (left) are smaller than females (right).

LET'S EXPLORE MATH

During the day, leaf chameleons live on the forest floor. At night, they move off the ground into trees.

Suppose a leaf chameleon is going to move 5 centimeters up a tree. So far, it has moved $\frac{4}{5}$ centimeter. How many more centimeters must it move? Use the area model to write an equation and find the solution.

King Croc

Crocodiles are the largest and heaviest reptiles alive. The saltwater crocodile of Australia is 20 feet (6 meters) in length and about 2,200 pounds (1,000 kilograms). Its great size makes it a predator to be feared!

As adults, these crocodiles are masters of their habitats. But while young, they are vulnerable. They must be closely protected by their mothers. At first, young crocodiles feed on small prey, such as snails, frogs, and insects. As they get bigger and stronger, their diets change. Fish and small **mammals** are now fair game.

Crocodiles are able to travel by both land and water. On land, they walk on all four legs. In the water, they swim by moving their tails back and forth. Like other crocodiles, their eyes are located high atop their snouts. This allows the reptile to **submerge** itself and still see above the water.

Some scientists believe that this species lives as a community like that of a wolf pack. In a group of crocodiles, there may be a dominant creature. This crocodile would likely be the **alpha** member of the group. He would have special privileges, like first choice of nesting spaces!

A saltwater crocodile hatches from an egg.

saltwater crocodile

Big Blue

The blue whale is an extraordinary creature. It is the biggest mammal of all time!

As the world's largest mammal, the whale weighs about 150 tons (136,000 kg). How heavy is that? Well, their tongues are about as heavy as a full-grown elephant!

At birth, blue whale calves are already about 26 ft. (8 m) long. That is longer than the height of a two-story building! For the first year of their lives, calves feed only on their mother's milk. Calves gain about 200 lb. (91 kg) a day during their first year!

Blue whales are **carnivores**. They live mostly on a diet of **krill**. To eat, they simply open their enormous mouths and take a huge gulp of water. Bristles, called **baleen**, filter the water without letting krill escape.

Blue whales travel alone and in groups. They are thought to communicate with loud groans. Scientists have varying opinions about the range in which blue whales can hear. Some scientists believe that they can hear up to 100 miles (161 kilometers) away. Other scientists believe that they can hear up to 1,000 mi. (1,609 km) away.

This blue whale is more than three times the size of the boat.

LET'S EXPLORE MATH

Tiny krill make up a big part of blue whale diets. Krill are so small, blue whales eat up to 40 million of them each day! Suppose that two krill weigh $\frac{9}{10}$ gram and $\frac{4}{5}$ gram.

1. Is the total weight of both krill greater than or less than 1 gram? How do you know?
2. What is the total weight of both krill? Write an equation using common denominators to show your solution.
3. How much more does one krill weigh than the other? Write an equation using common denominators to show your solution.

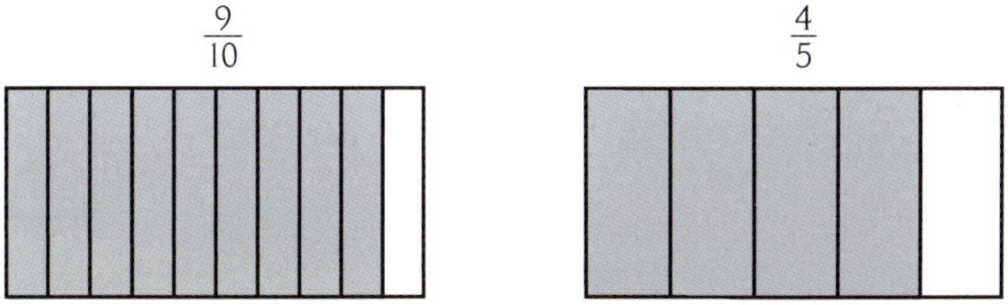

Slowpokes and Speedsters

The animal kingdom has fast and slow lanes. Some creatures **plod** along, traveling at oh-so-slow speeds. Other creatures are so fast they can't be caught. Let's explore some of the slowest and the fastest animals on Earth.

Sloths

Sloths are the world's slowest mammals, and they don't do much other than sleep. They are known to spend up to 20 hours a day snoozing. When they are awake, they move so slowly that their movements can barely be called activity! Because they are inactive much of the time, algae often grow on their fur. Algae are a type of simple, nonflowering plant. It gives sloths' fur a greenish tint.

Sloth species are not trying to be lazy. This behavior helps them survive. Sloths have an incredibly slow **digestive system**, and it can take them weeks to digest a single meal.

Because of this, sloths need to **conserve** their energy. In other words, a slow sloth is a healthy sloth!

Sloths spend their days in the trees, hanging from branches. On land, sloths get around by dragging themselves, which is not exactly the speediest way to travel.

Sloths are strong swimmers, moving three times faster in water than they do on land.

LET'S EXPLORE MATH

Imagine that scientists study the sleeping habits of two sloths. Sloth A sleeps for $\frac{5}{8}$ of a day. Sloth B sleeps for $\frac{5}{6}$ of a day.

1. Which sloth sleeps a greater fraction of a day? How do you know?
2. How much longer does one sloth sleep than the other? Explain your solution using words, numbers, or pictures.

sloth

Falcon vs. Hummingbird

There is some debate about which bird flies the fastest. The peregrine falcon is famously fast. At top speed, this bird flies over 200 mi. (322 km) per hour. But then, there are Anna's hummingbirds. Scientists believe that these little birds might even be quicker than falcons!

The Anna's hummingbird has been called "faster than a fighter jet." How can this be? According to research, these hummingbirds fly about 90 ft. (27 m) per second. That is slower than the peregrine falcon, which flies 229 ft. (70 m) per second. However, scientists argue that this comparison isn't fair since the falcon is so much bigger than the hummingbird.

If you look at how fast the two birds move according to their size, the results are a little different. The falcon moves 200 times its body lengths per second. Anna's hummingbird moves a whopping 385 body lengths per second. So, who's fastest? That depends on whom you ask!

Anna's hummingbird

peregrine falcon

Fast and Fierce Feline

Cheetahs have long been praised for their speed. They are able to dash as fast as 70 miles per hour (113 kilometers per hour), and they can even go from 0 to 60 mph (97 kph) in only three seconds! This makes the large, spotted cats the fastest animals on land.

Everyone knows that cheetahs are fast, but not many people know why. Cheetahs' bodies are made for top speed! They have tough paws that give them **traction**, or grip, to run across the flat landscape. Their **slender** limbs help them take long strides and their long tails keep them balanced while they run. Even their organs help them run faster. Their livers and hearts are big organs, giving them the strength they need to push their bodies to the limit.

Cheetahs usually do not need to reach top speeds when hunting. Their excellent eyesight helps them to zero in on their next meal. When they catch sight of their prey, it's time to start the chase. After closing in, cheetahs knock down their prey and bite their throats. But after all that hard work, cheetahs need about 30 minutes to **recover** before they eat.

A cheetah closes in on a jackal.

LET'S EXPLORE MATH

Imagine that two cheetah cubs are born at the zoo. One cub is $\frac{5}{16}$ pound. The other is $\frac{3}{8}$ pound.

1. Is the total weight of both cubs greater than or less than 1 pound? How do you know?
2. One of the veterinary assistants calculates the total weight of the cubs with the equation below. Explain why the answer is incorrect and find the correct total weight of the cubs.

$$\frac{5}{16} + \frac{3}{8} = \frac{8}{24}$$

Black lines near a cheetah's eyes help reflect sun glare when hunting.

Sneaky Creatures and Standout Stars

Some records are easy to award. The heaviest creatures weigh the most, and the lightest creatures weigh the least. There are also numbers to prove the winners. But it is hard to agree on which creatures are the most colorful or the sneakiest!

The winners of this category are **subjective**, or based on personal opinion. Some people may agree while others may not. Either way, it's hard to deny that these creatures are one of a kind!

Lilac-Breasted Roller

The lilac-breasted roller is one the world's most colorful birds. It is a sight to behold. The bird has its own unique hues. The roller features turquoise, electric blue, purple, pink, and green feathers.

This species may seem rare because of its unique colors, but in Africa, the bird is quite common. It makes its home in many countries in southern and eastern Africa. But, it is the national bird of Kenya.

Pictures do not do the bird justice. To truly understand the bird's charm, you must see it fly. While courting, the male birds fly in strange patterns. They "roll" through the air to try to get the attention of females!

A lilac-breasted roller flies above Kruger National Park in South Africa.

lilac-breasted roller

Poison Dart Frogs

Neon colors aren't often found in nature. Such bright hues are bound to stand out. In the poison dart frog's case, we are lucky that they stand out, because this frog is deadly. Its species got its name because tribes used the frog's poison to coat their arrows for hunting.

Dart frogs come in a variety of colors and designs, such as bright blue and neon yellow. Some poison dart frogs are spotted, and others are solid colors. There is likely to be a poison dart frog in your favorite color!

The frog's appearance is a form of protection. Its bright colors tell predators to stay away. Poison dart frogs release **toxic** venom through their skin. Some of the frogs are more dangerous than others. The golden dart frog is very toxic. In fact, the golden dart frog may be one of the most poisonous animals on the planet. It has enough poison to kill 10 adult men!

A Colombian man makes a poison arrow for hunting by touching its tip to the body of a golden dart frog.

blue dart frog

golden dart frog

green and black dart frog

LET'S EXPLORE MATH

Imagine that scientists are studying poison dart frogs in the rain forest. Of the frogs they see, $\frac{1}{3}$ are striped, $\frac{1}{2}$ are yellow, and the rest are blue. What fraction of the frogs that they see are blue? Use words, numbers, or pictures to explain your reasoning.

Leaf-Tailed Gecko

The leaf-tailed gecko is a master of camouflage. Like the *Brookesia micra* chameleon, it is a native of Madagascar.

These sneaky geckos are **nocturnal**. They are awake at night and sleep during the day. They prefer to sleep on tree trunks, where they blend in with the tree bark. Camouflaging allows them to hide from predators. The gecko's skin is rough and looks like the bark of a tree. At night, they hunt for insects—their food of choice.

leaf-tailed geckos

Scorpionfish

Scorpionfish make their homes in warm waters where there are plenty of coral reefs. Like the leaf-tailed gecko, they have a talent for blending in with their environment. This fish is usually found among the rocks and stones on the seafloor. Because of this, the fish is often called a stonefish. Scorpionfish can come in a variety of colors. Some of them are covered in fins and skin flaps that make them blend in with the coral.

The creature got its name because it stings like a scorpion. Their scariest features are their poisonous spines! Scorpionfish use them to protect themselves.

Animal Champs

The animal kingdom is made up of creatures of all sizes, shapes, and colors. They might be large or small, slow or fast. They might be sneaky and bright. Some might blend into the background, while others can't help but stand out.

For now, let's honor the current champs. But be aware, there are thousands of new animal species discovered each year. Some scientists estimate that 86 out of 100 land species and 91 out of 100 ocean species have yet to be discovered or named. The discovery of new species means that some of these creatures may make the record books. We just don't know about them yet.

Keep your eyes on the world of wildlife for new records to be set and broken.

Problem Solving

Imagine that scientists at a wildlife sanctuary are studying three sloths. They record the fraction of the day each sloth spends on certain activities. Use the table to answer the questions and summarize the data.

Sloth	Sleeping	Eating	Climbing or Hanging
1	$\frac{3}{4}$	$\frac{1}{12}$	$\frac{1}{6}$
2	$\frac{5}{6}$	$\frac{1}{24}$	$\frac{1}{8}$
3	$\frac{2}{3}$	$\frac{1}{24}$	$\frac{7}{24}$

1. Which sloth spends the greatest fraction of the day sleeping? How do you know?

2. Which sloth spends the greatest fraction of the day awake (eating and climbing or hanging)? How do you know?

3. What is the difference between the greatest and least fractions of the day that the sloths spend sleeping? Write an equation using common denominators to show your solution.

4. The scientists decide to be more specific, and list two fractions to show the parts of the day each sloth spends climbing and hanging. Match the data to the sloths.

   a. Climbing: $\frac{1}{24}$ Hanging: $\frac{1}{12}$

   b. Climbing: $\frac{7}{48}$ Hanging: $\frac{7}{48}$

   c. Climbing: $\frac{1}{24}$ Hanging: $\frac{1}{8}$

Glossary

alpha—the most powerful person or animal in a group

baleen—tough material in toothless whales' mouths used to remove food from seawater

carnivores—meat eaters

conserve—to use something carefully to prevent its loss or waste

echolocation—a process of locating distant objects, like prey, using reflected sound waves

digestive system—the body system that digests and processes food

habitats—places or environments where plants or animals live

insectivores—animals that eat insects

krill—very small ocean creatures that are the main food source of baleen whales

mammals—animals that are covered in hair or fur and feed milk to their young

nocturnal—active mainly during the night

plod—to walk slowly and heavily

recover—to return to a normal state

reptiles—cold-blooded animals whose bodies are covered in scales and who lay eggs

slender—narrow or thin

subjective—based on feelings or opinions

submerge—to go underwater

toxic—containing poisonous substances

traction—a force which causes things in motion to slow down

Index

Answer Key

Let's Explore Math

page 7:

1. Less than $\frac{1}{2}$ ounce; Explanations will vary but may include a comparison indicating that $\frac{1}{2}$ ounce is $\frac{50}{100}$, and the bumblebee bat weighs only $\frac{7}{100}$.
2. A; Explanations will vary but may include that since $\frac{7}{100}$ is closer to 0 than $\frac{1}{2}$, two bumblebee bats will not weigh more than $\frac{1}{2}$ ounce.

page 9:

$5 - \frac{4}{5} = 4\frac{1}{5}$; Area model should show $\frac{4}{5}$ crossed off.

page 13:

1. Greater than 1 gram; Explanations will vary but may include that $\frac{9}{10}$ and $\frac{4}{5}$ are both close to 1 whole, so when added, their sum must be greater than 1.
2. $\frac{9}{10} + \frac{8}{10} = \frac{17}{10}$ or $1\frac{7}{10}$
3. $\frac{9}{10} - \frac{8}{10} = \frac{1}{10}$

page 15:

1. Sloth B; Explanations will vary but may include using common denominators to write equivalent fractions or reasoning describing that $\frac{5}{6}$ is closer to 1 than $\frac{5}{8}$.
2. $\frac{5}{24}$; Explanations should show that $\frac{5}{6} - \frac{5}{8}$, or $\frac{20}{24} - \frac{15}{24}$, is $\frac{5}{24}$.

page 19:

1. Less than 1 pound; Explanations will vary but may include that $\frac{5}{16}$ and $\frac{3}{8}$ are both less than $\frac{1}{2}$, so when added, their sum must be less than 1.
2. The answer is incorrect because common denominators are not used and the original denominators are added; $\frac{5}{16} + \frac{3}{8}$, or $\frac{5}{16} + \frac{6}{16}$, is $\frac{11}{16}$ pound.

page 23:

$\frac{1}{6}$; Explanations should show that $\frac{1}{3} + \frac{1}{2}$, or $\frac{2}{6} + \frac{3}{6}$, is $\frac{5}{6}$. Therefore, $\frac{1}{6}$ must be blue because $\frac{5}{6} + \frac{1}{6} = \frac{6}{6}$ or 1.

Problem Solving

1. Sloth 2; Explanations will vary but may include using common denominators to write equivalent fractions.
2. Sloth 3; Explanations will vary but may include adding or subtracting to prove that Sloth 3 spends $\frac{8}{24}$, or $\frac{1}{3}$, of its day awake and comparing this fraction to the fractions of the day the other sloths are awake.
3. $\frac{1}{6}$ or equivalent fraction; $\frac{5}{6} - \frac{4}{6} = \frac{1}{6}$
4. **a.** Sloth 2
   b. Sloth 3
   c. Sloth 1